baby &
toddler

JODY VASSALLO

FORTIORI

HEALTHY EATING FOR BABIES AND TODDLERS

Introducing babies to the pleasures of healthy eating marks the beginning of an important stage in their development. A nutritious diet and regular exercise should be a high priority for parents, because they provide so many benefits, both immediate and long term. A healthy lifestyle will help children grow and develop properly and it also sets the foundations for healthy living as they get older. It will help them achieve their full physical and mental potential, and reduce their risk of weight gain and common diseases, such as heart disease and type 2 diabetes. Healthy eating and regular exercise should be a priority for the whole family.

The information in this book is intended for parents of healthy babies and toddlers and provides general guidelines about healthy eating for young children. It is not intended to replace any advice given to you by a qualified health professional regarding your child's dietary needs. The recipes are designed to cater for children aged from approximately 6 months to 3 years. 'First bites' are for babies aged from approximately 6 to 12 months.

During the first 12 months, babies grow and develop at a faster rate than at any other time in their lives. They need more nutrients per kilogram of their body weight than adults. Breast milk or a suitable formula should be their sole source of nutrition for the first 4 to 6 months. If possible, mothers should breastfeed their babies, rather than use a formula, particularly for the first 4 months of life. Breast milk contains many protective elements, which are not found in formulas, that help protect the baby's health and promote development. Breast milk or formula should remain an important part of a baby's diet for the first 12 months of life, although they will drink progressively less as they get older and start eating more solid food.

STARTING ON SOLID FOOD

Between 4 and 6 months of age, breast milk or formula can no longer meet all of a baby's nutritional needs, and babies need to start eating solid food in addition to regular breast milk or formula. Signs that babies are ready to start eating solids include: they can hold up their head; they want to feed more often; they start to watch other family members while they're eating; they lean forward and open their mouth or reach out if food is near; and they are more restless during the night. It's important not to introduce solids before a baby is developmentally ready, because it can damage a baby's digestive system and kidneys or precipitate a food allergy. On the other hand, solid food should not be introduced too late, because this can impair normal development and lead to problems with food acceptance. Later on it may also lead to iron deficiency, since breast milk or formula doesn't provide all of the iron a baby needs after 6 months of age. If you're having trouble deciding if your baby is ready for solid food, consult your doctor or child health nurse.

Dr Susanna Holt (PhD, dietitian)

4 to 6 months

The first food you introduce to your baby should be pureed or mashed to give it a soft, smooth texture. It's recommended that an iron-fortified, rice-based infant cereal, mixed with breast milk or infant formula, is the first food you introduce, because it is easily digested and rarely causes an allergic reaction. Start by introducing a small amount of rice cereal paste (1/2-1 teaspoon) once a day after a breast or bottle feed when your baby is relatively relaxed. Only small amounts of food are needed at this time to get your baby used to eating. Gradually increase the amount offered to 1-2 tablespoons. After 2 to 3 weeks of rice cereal, you can start to offer cooked, pureed fruit and vegetables, such as peeled apple, pear, banana, potato and pumpkin. Only offer one new food at a time so that you can determine whether or not your baby is allergic to any particular food. If your baby has had no reaction after 3 to 4 days, it is safe to introduce another new food. Additional seasonings, such as salt and sugar, should not be added to a baby's food, because they can put a strain on their immature kidneys.

Always supervise babies when they are eating in case they experience any problems, such as choking. If you have a family history of any type of food allergy or serious food intolerance, particularly to nuts, eggs, fish, wheat, meat or cow's milk, consult your doctor for advice before you begin to introduce any solid food to your baby's diet.

INTRODUCING SOLIDS: The First Steps

| **Week 1** Start with 1/2-1 teaspoon of moist rice cereal once a day after a breast or bottle feed. Gradually increase the amount.
| **Week 2** Increase to 2 rice cereal feeds a day after breast or bottle feeds.
| **Week 3** Add cooked pureed soft fruit, such as apple, pear or banana, to 1 of the 2 rice cereal meals. Introduce 1 new food at a time.
| **Week 4** Add pureed vegetables, such as well-cooked potato, carrots, zucchini (courgette) or pumpkin, as a third meal per day.
| **From week 5** Continue to offer a variety of blander fruit and vegetables, gradually increasing the amount to 1/2 cup (125 ml/ 4 fl oz) of solids per meal.

Table adapted from: Feeding your baby solid foods. The facts. A pamphlet produced by Golden Circle Ltd, 2002.

---

7 to 9 months

From between 7 and 9 months of age, you can offer your baby solids before a breast or bottle feed. At this age, a baby may eat 2 to 3 meals of rice cereal with fruit and vegetables, plus 3 to 5 breast or bottle feeds each day. Meals will consist of 1/3-1/2 cup (80-125 ml/$2^2/3$-4 fl oz) of food. Your baby should now be eating food with a coarser, lumpier texture, such as fork-mashed or finely chopped food. Offer a variety of food with different textures and tastes to promote the nerve and muscle stimulation needed for normal speech development. Offer a variety of differently coloured fruit and vegetables each week to provide a range of healthy nutrients and to tempt the appetite. Iron-rich food, such as finely minced meats and iron-fortified cereals, should be a regular part of your baby's diet.

SUITABLE FOODS BETWEEN 7 AND 9 MONTHS OF AGE

I **Cereal products** Products based on rice, wheat or oats can be offered, such as baby muesli, pasta and bread. Baby rusks and pieces of toast can also be offered to promote chewing, but supervise babies while they are eating, in case they start to choke. If you have a family history of wheat allergy, delay the introduction of wheat until at least 12 months, and consult your doctor beforehand.

I **Fruit** Soft, peeled fruit, sliced or coarsely pureed, is suitable (banana, melon, pear, avocado). Fruit juice is not necessary and shouldn't be a regular feature of a baby's diet. Diluted unsweetened fruit juice can be offered occasionally to encourage drinking, but it should be limited to less than 1/2 cup (125 ml/ 4 fl oz) per day.

I **Vegetables** Peeled vegetables, cooked until they are soft, and then coarsely mashed or finely chopped, are suitable (pumpkin, sweet potato, potato, zucchini/courgette, carrot, broccoli). Offer a variety of differently coloured vegetables each week and try not to serve the same vegetables on a daily basis.

I **Dairy products** Breast milk or infant formula should continue to be a baby's main drink for the first year. Cooked custards and yoghurts can be offered at this stage. Choose calcium-enriched soy versions if your baby has problems with cow's milk. (If you have a family history of soy allergy, consult your doctor before feeding your baby any soy products.) Grated mild cheddar cheese or cottage cheese can also be added to meals. Low-fat dairy products are not necessary for at least the first 2 years of life.

I **Eggs** Cooked egg yolk can be introduced from 7 to 9 months of age, and if tolerated, cooked egg white can be introduced from 10 months of age. If you have a family history of egg allergy, delay the introduction of egg until 12 months, and consult your doctor beforehand.

I **Meat and alternatives** After your baby's teeth have started appearing, you can introduce well-cooked chicken, lean red meat, and boneless fish (in that order). These foods should be minced, coarsely pureed or finely chopped, and all bones and gristle should be removed. Tofu and well-cooked, mashed lentils or beans can be introduced at this stage. If you have a family history of fish or soy allergy, delay the introduction of these foods until 12 months, and consult your doctor beforehand.

9 to 12 months

Between 9 and 12 months of age, babies consume an average of 2 to 4 breast or bottle feeds and 3 meals per day. Each meal consists of about 3/4-1 cup (185-250 ml/ 6-8 fl oz) of food. At this stage, babies should be trying to feed themselves with finger food or a soft spoon. By 10 months, water and diluted pure fruit juice can be offered. Limit juice to no more than 1/2 cup (125 ml/4 fl oz) once a day. Meals should contain a variety of food from the different food groups: cereal products; fruit or vegetables; and protein-rich food (meat, chicken, fish, eggs, dairy products or baked beans). Food should be finger food (toast fingers, cooked broccoli florets, pieces of soft fruit) or food that is roughly mashed and chopped. Mixed meals such as pasta dishes, casseroles and omelettes can be served. Incorporate some of the food the rest of the family eat into your baby's meals.

HEALTHY EATING FOR TODDLERS

Toddlers between 1 and 2 years of age can enjoy a varied diet, including many of the meals and food eaten by the rest of the family. However, during this time of life, eating patterns can become a little erratic. Toddlers are often more hungry during their growth spurts than at other times. Research has shown that, if left to their own devices and given access to a range of healthy food, toddlers are quite good at selecting an adequate diet. So don't be alarmed if they don't seem to be eating very much for a while - they are likely to make up for it later on. Don't try to force them to eat when they are clearly not interested. However, consult your doctor if your toddler has little appetite and hasn't been eating well for more than a few days.

Like adults, toddlers require a varied and balanced diet that contains all the major food groups. Their diet should be largely based on fruit, vegetables, legumes and grain products, with moderate amounts of protein-rich foods (eggs, full-fat dairy products, meat, chicken and fish). Toddlers and young children are still growing and developing rapidly and require plenty of energy and nutrients, but they only have small stomachs, so they need to be getting more nutrients per mouthful. Low-fat diets are not suitable for children under 5 years of age (unless advised by a doctor), because an adequate fat intake is essential for providing sufficient calories and is needed for the normal development of nerves, eyes and the brain. Dietary fat should be obtained from nutritious sources rather than 'junk' food. Good-quality sources of fat include full-fat dairy products, eggs enriched with omega-3 fat, salmon, tuna, chicken and red meat. A high-fibre diet is also not appropriate for young children, because it may prevent them from eating enough calories and absorbing certain nutrients.

Mobile toddlers usually require 3 meals plus snacks each day to keep them adequately fuelled. A meal or snack should be offered every 2 to 3 hours. It's good to maintain a consistent pattern from day to day, because toddlers feel more secure when they know what to expect. Snacks should mostly consist of wholesome foods, in order to meet the toddler's high nutrient requirements. Less nutritious snacks, such as confectionery and potato chips or crisps, should not be a regular feature of a toddler's diet, because they tend to replace more healthy food and can leave the child short of certain nutrients. As well as regular meals and snacks, toddlers need plenty of water throughout the day. Always take a water bottle with you when you go out, so that you can keep your toddler well hydrated when away from home.

A guide to feeding your toddler food from the 4 main food groups each day

| **Fruit and vegetables** (fresh, frozen, canned or dried) 3 to 5 serves per day

| **Cereal products and starchy vegetables** (such as bread, pasta, rice, potatoes and corn) 3 to 4 serves per day

| **Meat and alternatives** (poultry, fish, eggs and legumes) 1 to 2 serves per day

| **Dairy products** 2 to 3 serves per day

TAKE ONE, ADD SOME

apple & oatmeal pureed
with ricotta

lamb & vegetables pureed
with gnocchi

egg custard pureed
with peaches in natural juice

tuna & vegetables pureed
with couscous

berry yoghurt dessert pureed
with softened wheat biscuit

pear & banana pureed
with yoghurt

udon noodles pureed
with pumpkin & sweet corn

avocado pureed with
prepared baby rice cereal

vegetables & lentils pureed
with rice pasta

banana custard pureed
with creamed rice & sultanas

pumpkin & sweet corn pureed
with ricotta & spinach pasta

chicken & vegetables pureed
with butter beans

Try these easy ideas when you need to prepare a quick meal. Simply take a jar of commercial baby food and puree it with the other ingredients suggested.

Commercial baby foods are a useful standby, but home-cooked foods should be the mainstay of a child's diet. When possible, feed your baby home-cooked meals without added sugar and salt. Home-cooked meals tend to have a range of different textures and natural flavours, which offer more stimulation. Cooking a large batch of food and then freezing mini portions of pureed or mashed food in ice cube trays is a great way to save time. It is particularly useful early on when your baby only needs 1 cube per meal.

FIRST BITES

easy chicken vegetable soup

EASY CHICKEN VEGETABLE SOUP

1 medium skinless chicken thigh
  fillet, chopped
1 cup (100 g/3⅓ oz) mixed frozen
  vegetables (carrots, cauliflower,
  peas, beans)
2 cups (500 ml/16 fl oz)
  reduced-salt chicken stock
2 tablespoons white rice

1 Put the chicken, vegetables and stock into a pan and bring to the boil, then reduce the heat.

2 Add the rice, cover and simmer for 30 minutes or until the chicken is tender. Remove from the heat and set aside to cool slightly.

3 Puree the soup in batches in a blender or food processor until smooth. Makes 2½ cups (625 ml/ 20 fl oz)

per cup (250 ml/8 fl oz) | fat 7.7 g | saturated fat 2.5 g | protein 21.2 g | carbohydrate 14.2 g | fibre 2.5 g | cholesterol 81 mg | energy 901 kJ (215 Cal)

POTATO & BABY PEA PUREE

500 g (1 lb) potatoes, peeled and
  roughly chopped
1½ cups (375 ml/12 fl oz) water
1 cup (150 g/5 oz) fresh or frozen
  baby peas
1 tablespoon infant formula
  powder

1 Put the potatoes and water into a pan and bring to the boil. Reduce the heat, cover and simmer for 30 minutes.

2 Add the peas, cover and cook for 5 minutes or until the potatoes are soft. Remove from the heat and set aside to cool slightly.

3 Puree the vegetables, cooking liquid and baby formula in batches in a food processor or blender until smooth. Makes 2 cups (500 ml/16 fl oz)

per cup (250 ml/8 fl oz) | fat 1.7 g | saturated fat 0.5 g | protein 10.9 g | carbohydrate 42.6 g | fibre 8.2 g | cholesterol 1 mg | energy 1049 kJ (250 Cal)

* Refrigerate or freeze the puree in serving-sized portions in heatproof airtight containers. Thaw completely, then reheat by standing the container in a bowl of boiling water.

potato & baby pea purée

BAKED BANANA CUSTARD POTS

2 small ripe bananas
3 eggs, lightly beaten
**1½ cups (375 ml/12 fl oz) milk or
reconstituted infant formula**

1 Preheat oven to 170°C (325°F/Gas 3).
2 Put the bananas into a blender or food processor and blend until smooth.
3 Add the eggs and milk and blend until creamy. Divide the mixture among 6 x ½ cup (125 ml/4 fl oz) capacity ramekins.
4 Put the ramekins into a baking dish and pour in enough boiling water to come halfway up the sides of the ramekins.
5 Bake for 15-20 minutes or until the custard is set. Set aside to cool slightly before serving. Serves 6

per serve I **fat 5 g** I **saturated fat 2.4 g** I **protein 5.8 g** I **carbohydrate 8.5 g** I **fibre 0.6 g** I **cholesterol 102 mg** I **energy 425 kJ (101 Cal)**

* This recipe is suitable for babies from 10 months of age.

baked banana custard pots

muffin rusks with avocado

MUFFIN RUSKS WITH AVOCADO

1 Toast the muffin until golden brown. Spread the muffin with the butter or margarine.
2 Mash the avocado and spread onto the muffin. Cut into fingers. Serves 1

per serve | **fat 11.4 g** | **saturated fat 3.3 g** | **protein 3.9 g** | **carbohydrate 11.9 g** | **fibre 1.6 g** | **cholesterol 6 mg** | **energy 703 kJ (167 Cal)**

½ **English muffin**
½ **teaspoon butter or margarine**
¼ **small avocado**

STEWED PEARS & APRICOTS

1 Put the pears, apricots and water into a pan and bring to the boil. Reduce the heat, cover and simmer for 15 minutes or until the pears are very soft. Remove from the heat and set aside to cool slightly.
2 Drain the pears and apricots and puree in a blender or food processor until smooth. Makes 1 cup (250 ml/ 8 fl oz)

per cup (250 ml/8 fl oz) | **fat 0.4 g** | **saturated fat 0 g** | **protein 1.9 g** | **carbohydrate 51.5 g** | **fibre 7.7 g** | **cholesterol 0 mg** | **energy 938 kJ (223 Cal)**

* You could use apples or peaches instead of pears. If you are short of time, try using canned pears in natural juice. Chill the cooking liquid and serve it to your child for a refreshing drink.

2 **medium pears, peeled, cored and chopped***
6 **dried apricot halves**
2 **cups (500 ml/16 fl oz) water**

stewed pears & apricots

semolina with apple

SEMOLINA WITH APPLE

1 tablespoon semolina
1 cup (250 ml/8 fl oz) milk or
    reconstituted infant formula
1 tablespoon apple puree

1 Put the semolina and milk or baby formula into a pan and stir over medium heat for 5 minutes or until the semolina is thick and soft.

2 Spoon the semolina into a serving bowl and gently swirl through the apple puree. Set aside to cool slightly before serving. Serves 1

per serve | fat 9.5 g | saturated fat 5.2 g | protein 7.4 g | carbohydrate 24.9 g | fibre 0.9 g | cholesterol 22 mg | energy 901 kJ (214 Cal)

CARROT, PARSNIP & CHICKPEA PUREE

500 g (1 lb) carrots, peeled and
    roughly chopped
250 g (8 oz) parsnips, peeled and
    roughly chopped
2 cups (500 ml/16 fl oz) water
400 g (13 oz) can chickpeas,
    rinsed and drained

1 Put the carrots, parsnips and water into a large pan and bring to the boil. Reduce the heat, cover and simmer for 20 minutes.

2 Add the chickpeas, cover and cook for 10 minutes or until the vegetables are very soft. Remove from the heat and set aside to cool slightly.

3 Puree the vegetables, chickpeas and cooking liquid in batches in a food processor or blender until smooth. Makes 4 cups (1 litre/32 fl oz)

per cup (250 ml/8 fl oz) | fat 1.5 g | saturated fat 0.2 g | protein 5.9 g | carbohydrate 21.1 g | fibre 8 g | cholesterol 0 mg | energy 570 kJ (136 Cal)

* Refrigerate or freeze the puree in serving-sized portions in heatproof airtight containers. Thaw completely, then reheat by standing the container in a bowl of boiling water.

carrot, parsnip & chickpea puree

creamy banana rice

CREAMY BANANA RICE

1 Put the milk into a pan, add the vanilla and heat until it is just about to boil.

2 Add the rice and stir for 1 minute or until the mixture returns to the boil. Reduce the heat to low and simmer for 30 minutes, stirring occasionally, until the rice is tender.

3 Stir in the bananas and sultanas. Set aside to cool slightly before serving. Serves 2-4

per serve (4) I fat 5 g I saturated fat 3.2 g I protein 6.1 g I carbohydrate 29.5 g I fibre 1.4 g I cholesterol 17 mg I energy 788 kJ (188 Cal)

* Store any leftover banana rice in the fridge in an airtight container. Delicious served hot or cold.

2 cups (500 ml/16 fl oz) milk
1/2 teaspoon vanilla essence
1/4 cup (55 g/1 2/3 oz) arborio rice
2 medium ripe bananas, mashed
1 tablespoon sultanas, finely chopped

PUMPKIN COUSCOUS PUREE

½ cup (95 g/3 oz) couscous
1 cup (250 ml/8 fl oz) boiling water
350 g (12 oz) peeled Jap pumpkin,
   chopped
1 cup (250 ml/8 fl oz) water
1 medium zucchini (courgette),
   chopped

1 Put the couscous into a bowl, cover with the boiling water and set aside for 10 minutes or until all the liquid has been absorbed.

2 Put the pumpkin and water into a pan and bring to the boil. Reduce the heat, cover and cook for 10 minutes.

3 Add the zucchini and cook for 5 minutes or until the vegetables are very soft. Remove from the heat and set aside to cool slightly.

4 Puree the vegetables, cooking liquid and couscous in batches in a food processor or blender until smooth.
Makes 2½ cups (625 ml/20 fl oz)

per cup (250 ml/8 fl oz) | **fat 0.9 g** | **saturated fat 0.5 g** | **protein 8.3 g** | **carbohydrate 38.7 g** | **fibre 2.7 g** | **cholesterol 0 mg** | **energy 853 kJ (203 Cal)**

* Refrigerate or freeze the puree in serving-sized portions in heatproof airtight containers. Thaw completely, then reheat by standing the container in a bowl of boiling water.

pumpkin couscous puree

sweet potato & broccoli puree

SWEET POTATO & BROCCOLI PUREE

1 Put the sweet potato and water into a pan and bring to the boil. Reduce the heat, cover and simmer for 10 minutes.

2 Add the broccoli and cook for 5 minutes or until the vegetables are very soft. Remove from the heat and set aside to cool slightly.

3 Puree the vegetables and cooking liquid in batches in a food processor or blender until smooth. Makes 2½ cups (625 ml/20 fl oz)

per cup (250 ml/8 fl oz) I **fat 0.4 g** I **saturated fat 0 g** I **protein 7.6 g** I **carbohydrate 28.7 g** I **fibre 6.9 g** I **cholesterol 0 mg** I **energy 684 kJ (163 Cal)**

* Refrigerate or freeze the puree in serving-sized portions in heatproof airtight containers. Thaw completely, then reheat by standing the container in a bowl of boiling water.

500 g (1 lb) orange sweet potato, peeled and chopped
1 cup (250 ml/8 fl oz) water
200 g (6½ oz) broccoli, cut into florets

TODDLER BREAKFASTS

yoghurt with fruit & muesli

YOGHURT WITH FRUIT & MUESLI

½ cup (125 g/4 oz) plain yoghurt
140 g (4½ oz) apple puree
2 tablespoons natural (untoasted)
   muesli
2 strawberries, halved
½ kiwifruit, cut into wedges
100 g (3⅓ oz) pawpaw,
   thickly sliced

1 Put the yoghurt into a serving pot and swirl through the apple puree and muesli.
2 Serve the yoghurt accompanied with the strawberries, kiwifruit and pawpaw. Serves 2

per serve I fat 3 g I saturated fat 1.5 g I protein 4.7 g I carbohydrate 20.2 g I fibre 5.3 g I cholesterol 10 mg I energy 587 kJ (140 Cal)

BABY HAM & CHEESE MUFFINS

canola oil spray
1 cup (125 g/4 oz) self-raising
   flour
2 tablespoons unprocessed
   wheat bran
½ cup (60 g/2 oz) grated
   cheddar cheese
100 g (3⅓ oz) sliced ham,
   chopped
½ cup (125 ml/4 fl oz) milk
60 g (2 oz) butter, melted
1 egg, lightly beaten

1 Preheat oven to 200°C (400°F/Gas 6). Lightly spray 12 mini muffin holes with canola oil spray.
2 Sift the flour and bran into a bowl and stir in the cheese and ham. Make a well in the center.
3 Whisk together the milk, butter and egg, pour into the well and mix until just combined (the mixture should still be lumpy).
4 Divide the mixture among the muffin holes and bake for 10-15 minutes or until the muffins have risen. Makes 12

per muffin I fat 7.2 g I saturated fat 4.3 g I protein 4.9 g I carbohydrate 8 g I fibre 0.8 g I cholesterol 39 mg I energy 492 kJ (117 Cal)
* Freeze the muffins in an airtight container or sealed plastic bag for up to 1 month.

baby ham & cheese muffins

sweet corn scrambled googeys

SWEET CORN SCRAMBLED GOOGEYS

1 Whisk together the egg, milk, creamed corn and grated cheese.
2 Melt the butter or margarine in a non-stick fry pan over medium heat, add the egg mixture and cook for 3 minutes or until the egg starts to set around the edge. Stir gently with a wooden spoon to scramble and cook for 1 minute.
3 Serve the scrambled egg with toasted soldiers.
Serves 1
per serve | fat 18.4 g | saturated fat 9.7 g | protein 13.1 g | carbohydrate 22.4 g | fibre 2.3 g | cholesterol 225 mg | energy 1298 kJ (309 Cal)

- **1 egg, lightly beaten**
- **1 tablespoon milk**
- **2 tablespoons creamed corn**
- **1 tablespoon grated cheddar cheese**
- **10 g (1/3 oz) butter or margarine**
- **1 slice white bread, toasted and cut into thin strips**

FRUITY COUSCOUS

1 Put the apple and blackcurrant juice into a pan and bring to the boil. Pour over the couscous and set aside for 10 minutes or until the liquid has been absorbed.
2 Separate the couscous grains with a fork. Gently fold through the blueberries, raspberries and grapes.
3 Serve the couscous in bowls with the strawberry yoghurt. Serves 1-2
per serve (2) | fat 0.5 g | saturated fat 0.2 g | protein 3.9 g | carbohydrate 31.6 g | fibre 1.6 g | cholesterol 1 mg | energy 634 kJ (151 Cal)
* Store leftover fruity couscous in the refrigerator in an airtight container for up to 2 days.

- **1/2 cup (125 ml/4 fl oz) apple and blackcurrant juice**
- **1/4 cup (45 g/1 1/2 oz) couscous**
- **1/4 cup (40 g/1 1/3 oz) blueberries**
- **1/4 cup (30 g/1 oz) raspberries**
- **1/4 cup (45 g/1 1/2 oz) seedless green grapes, halved**
- **1 tablespoon no-added sugar strawberry yoghurt**

fruity couscous

zucchini omelette

ZUCCHINI OMELETTE

1 teaspoon butter or margarine
1 egg, lightly beaten
1/2 small zucchini (courgette),
    finely grated
1 tablespoon grated cheddar
    cheese

1 Melt the butter or margarine in a small non-stick fry pan over medium heat, add the egg and swirl to coat the base of the pan.

2 Sprinkle the egg with the grated zucchini and cheese. Cook for 2 minutes or until set, then turn over and cook the other side.

3 Remove the omelette from the pan and set aside to cool slightly before rolling up and cutting into slices. Serves 1

per serve | fat 12.3 g | saturated fat 6.2 g | protein 9.1 g | carbohydrate 0.5 g | fibre 0.3 g | cholesterol 209 mg | energy 620 kJ (148 Cal)

RASPBERRY-FILLED MUESLI MUFFINS

canola oil spray
1 cup (125 g/4 oz) self-raising
    flour
3 tablespoons brown sugar
1/2 cup (125 ml/4 fl oz) milk
60 g (2 oz) butter, melted
1 egg, lightly beaten
2 tablespoons raspberry no-added
    sugar fruit spread
2 tablespoons natural (untoasted)
    muesli

1 Preheat oven to 200°C (400°F/Gas 6). Lightly spray 12 mini muffin holes with canola oil spray.

2 Sift the flour into a bowl, stir in the sugar and make a well in the center.

3 Whisk together the milk, butter and egg, pour into the well and mix until just combined (the mixture should still be lumpy).

4 Divide half the mixture among the muffin holes. Spoon a little raspberry fruit spread into the center of each hole and top with the remaining muffin mixture. Sprinkle with the muesli and bake for 15 minutes or until the muffins have risen. Set aside for 15 minutes to allow the filling to cool before serving. Makes 12

per muffin | fat 5.3 g | saturated fat 3.2 g | protein 2.1 g | carbohydrate 13.2 g | fibre 0.6 g | cholesterol 30 mg | energy 454 kJ (108 Cal)

* Freeze the muffins in an airtight container or sealed plastic bag for up to 1 month.

raspberry-filled muesli muffins

cheesy baked bean bread cup

CHEESY BAKED BEAN BREAD CUP

1 Preheat oven to 220°C (425°F/Gas 7).

2 Brush both sides of the bread with the olive oil and press into a ½ cup (125 ml/4 fl oz) capacity muffin hole. Bake for 10 minutes or until the bread is crisp and golden.

3 Heat the baked beans in a pan over low heat until just warm.

4 Spoon the baked beans into the bread cup and sprinkle with the grated cheese. Serves 1

per serve | fat 13.9 g | saturated fat 3.6 g | protein 10.8 g | carbohydrate 27.9 g | fibre 6.8 g | cholesterol 10 mg | energy 1225 kJ (292 Cal)

1 thick slice white hi-fibre bread, crust removed

2 teaspoons olive oil

100 g (3⅓ oz) baked beans

1 tablespoon grated cheddar cheese

STRAWBERRY FRENCH TOAST

2 thick slices white hi-fibre bread
2 teaspoons strawberry no-added
sugar fruit spread
1 egg, lightly beaten
¼ cup (60 ml/2 fl oz) milk
10 g (⅓ oz) butter or margarine

1 Spread 1 piece of bread with the strawberry fruit spread. Top with the other piece of bread.
2 Whisk together the egg and milk in a shallow bowl.
3 Dip the sandwich into the egg mixture. Drain off any excess.
4 Melt the butter or margarine in a non-stick fry pan over medium heat. Cook the bread for 3 minutes each side or until golden brown.
5 Remove from the pan and use a cookie cutter to cut the French toast into shapes. Serves 1

per serve | **fat 18 g** | **saturated fat 8.9 g** | **protein 16.2 g** | **carbohydrate 40.8 g** | **fibre 4.1 g** | **cholesterol 221 mg** | **energy 1656 kJ (394 Cal)**

strawberry french toast

sunshine egg

SUNSHINE EGG

1 Use a large star-shaped cutter to cut out the center of the bread.

2 Melt the butter or margarine in a non-stick fry pan over medium heat. Place the bread in the center of the pan, add the star shape and cook for 2-3 minutes or until the bread is crisp and golden, then turn over.

3 Crack the egg into the center of the bread and cook for 3-5 minutes or until the egg has set.

Serves 1

per serve | fat 10.1 g | saturated fat 4.3 g | protein 10.2 g | carbohydrate 16.9 g | fibre 2 g | cholesterol 200 mg | energy 847 kJ (202 Cal)

1 thick slice white hi-fibre bread
1 teaspoon butter or margarine
1 egg

ALMOND PORRIDGE WITH APRICOTS

¼ cup (25 g/1 oz) rolled oats
1 tablespoon wheatgerm
1 tablespoon almond meal
1 cup (250 ml/8 fl oz) water
2 tablespoons milk
140 g (4½ oz) tub apricots in
   natural juice

1 Put the rolled oats, wheatgerm, almond meal and water into a pan over medium heat. Cook, stirring, for 3-5 minutes or until the oats are soft.
2 Spoon the porridge into a bowl and pour in the milk.
3 Drain the apricots, reserving the juice. Chop the apricots and sprinkle over the porridge with the reserved juice. Serves 1

per serve | fat 8.8 g | saturated fat 1.8 g | protein 8.2 g | carbohydrate 32.6 g | fibre 6.2 g | cholesterol 5 mg | energy 1068 kJ (254 Cal)

almond porridge with apricots

TODDLER
LUNCHES & SNACKS

hummus

VEGETABLE STICKS WITH AVOCADO HUMMUS

1/2 small zucchini (courgette),
  cut into sticks
1/2 medium avocado
2 tablespoons hummus
1 tablespoon plain yoghurt
1/2 small carrot, cut into sticks
1/2 celery stick, cut into sticks
1/4 small red capsicum (bell
  pepper), cut into sticks

1 Steam the zucchini until tender. Set aside to cool.
2 Mash the avocado and combine with the hummus and yoghurt. Serve the dip in a bowl and accompany with the vegetable sticks. Serves 1-2

per serve (2) | fat 14.9 g | saturated fat 3.3 g | protein 3.8 g | carbohydrate 4 g | fibre 3.4 g | cholesterol 2 mg | energy 715 kJ (170 Cal)

BANANA SOY SMOOTHIE

1 small banana
1 tablespoon plain yoghurt
1 teaspoon honey
1 cup (250 ml/8 fl oz) vanilla
  soy milk

1 Put the banana into a blender.
2 Add the yoghurt, honey and soy milk and blend until smooth. Serves 1-2

per serve (2) | fat 4.4 g | saturated fat 0.6 g | protein 5 g | carbohydrate 21.2 g | fibre 1.5 g | cholesterol 2 mg | energy 609 kJ (145 Cal)

banana soy smoothie

quesadillas with ham, cheese & tomato

QUESADILLAS WITH HAM, CHEESE & TOMATO

1 Lay 1 tortilla on a flat surface. Top with the ham, cheese, tomato and the remaining tortilla.
2 Lightly spray a non-stick fry pan with olive oil spray, add the tortilla stack and weigh it down with a plate. Cook over medium heat for 2 minutes or until the bottom tortilla is crisp and golden.
3 Slide the tortilla out of the pan and onto a plate. Return to the pan and cook the other side until it is crisp and golden and the cheese has melted. Cut into wedges to serve. Serves 1-2
per serve (2) | fat 5.6 g | saturated fat 2.5 g | protein 7.5 g | carbohydrate 11.1 g | fibre 1.3 g | cholesterol 17.3 mg | energy 537 kJ (128 Cal)

2 small flour tortillas (20 cm/8 in)
30 g (1 oz) shaved ham
2 tablespoons grated cheddar
  cheese
1 small tomato, sliced
olive oil spray

AVOCADO & TUNA RICE CAKES

1 Mash the avocado and stir in the tuna and carrot.
2 Spread the avocado mixture over the rice cake. Serves 1
per serve | fat 12 g | saturated fat 2.7 g | protein 8.1 g | carbohydrate 8.6 g | fibre 1.7 g | cholesterol 13 mg | energy 743 kJ (177 Cal)

1/4 small avocado
1 tablespoon tuna in springwater,
  drained
1 tablespoon grated carrot
1 rice cake

avocado & tuna rice cakes

oatmeal & sultana cookies

OATMEAL & SULTANA COOKIES

125 g (4 oz) butter or margarine

½ cup (115 g/3⅔ oz) firmly
  packed brown sugar

1 egg, lightly beaten

1 teaspoon vanilla essence

1 cup (125 g/4 oz) plain flour

1 teaspoon baking powder

1 cup (125 g/4 oz) fine oatmeal

1 cup (160 g/5⅓ oz) sultanas

1 Preheat oven to 180°C (350°F/Gas 4). Line 2 baking trays with baking paper.

2 Beat the butter or margarine and brown sugar in a bowl until light and creamy. Add the egg and vanilla essence and beat until combined.

3 Sift in the flour and baking powder and mix to combine. Add the oatmeal and sultanas and mix to form a soft dough.

4 Roll tablespoons of the mixture into balls. Place on the prepared trays and flatten slightly. Bake for 20-25 minutes or until golden. Makes about 20

per cookie I fat 6 g I saturated fat 3.6 g I protein 1.9 g I carbohydrate 20 g I fibre 1 g I cholesterol 25 mg I energy 594 kJ (141 Cal)

SIMPLE TUNA SALAD

2 tablespoons tuna in springwater,
  drained

½ celery stick, chopped

1 tablespoon corn kernels

1 tablespoon mayonnaise

1 large iceberg lettuce leaf,
  shredded

½ medium carrot, sliced

¼ small red capsicum (bell
  pepper), sliced

¼ medium Lebanese cucumber,
  sliced

1 hard-boiled egg, quartered

1 Combine the tuna, celery, corn and mayonnaise in a small bowl. Place the bowl on a plate.

2 Arrange the lettuce, carrot, capsicum, cucumber and egg to the side. Serves 1-2

per serve (2) I fat 6.1 g I saturated fat 1.3 g I protein 6.5 g I carbohydrate 4.4 g I fibre 1.3 g I cholesterol 115 mg I energy 420 kJ (100 Cal)

simple tuna salad

bubble & squeak

BUBBLE & SQUEAK

1 Melt the butter or margarine in a fry pan over medium heat.
2 Add the meat and vegetables to the pan and cook for 5 minutes or until heated through. Serves 1
per serve I fat 22 g I saturated fat 10.4 g I protein 35 g I carbohydrate 28.4 g I fibre 7.1 g I cholesterol 97 mg I **energy 1950 kJ (464 Cal)**
* This is a great meal to utilise roast dinner leftovers. Any roasted meat or vegetables can be used. It is delicious with leftover cauliflower in cheese sauce.

10 g (⅓ oz) butter or margarine
½ cup (95 g/3 oz) chopped
  cooked roast beef, lamb
  or chicken
1 piece baked potato, chopped
1 piece baked pumpkin, chopped
1 piece baked carrot, chopped
¼ cup (40 g/1⅓ oz) cooked peas

CAROB, DATE & APRICOT BALLS

1 Put the dates, apricots, sunflower seeds, pepitas, coconut and carob powder into a food processor and process to form a stiff paste. Transfer the mixture to a bowl.
2 Roll heaped teaspoons of the mixture into small balls then roll in the extra coconut. Shake off any excess coconut. Makes 20
per ball I fat 3.8 g I saturated fat 2.8 g I protein 1 g I carbohydrate 6.9 g I fibre 1.9 g I cholesterol 0 mg I **energy 287 kJ (68 Cal)**
* Carob powder is available from health-food shops or the health-food section of supermarkets. Refrigerate the balls in an airtight container for up to 1 week.

1 cup (195 g/6½ oz) fresh dates,
  pitted and roughly chopped
1 cup (135 g/4½ oz) dried
  apricots, roughly chopped
2 tablespoons sunflower seeds
1 tablespoon pepitas
1 tablespoon desiccated coconut
2 tablespoons carob powder*
1 cup (90 g/3 oz) desiccated
  coconut, extra, for rolling

carob, date & apricot balls

rainbow ice blocks

RAINBOW ICE BLOCKS

200 g (6½ oz) strawberries
2 cups (500 ml/16 fl oz) fresh
orange juice
½ cup (125 ml/4 fl oz)
passionfruit pulp

1 Put the strawberries into a blender or food processor and blend until smooth. Divide the strawberry puree among 8 x ⅓ cup (80 ml/ 2⅔ fl oz) capacity ice block moulds.
2 Combine the orange juice and passionfruit pulp and carefully pour into the ice block moulds. Add the sticks and freeze until firm.
3 Rub a warm cloth over the outside of each ice block hole and gently pull the stick to remove. Makes 8

per ice block | fat 0.1 g | saturated fat 0 g | protein 1.2 g | carbohydrate 6.4 g | fibre 2.8 g | cholesterol 0 mg | energy 163 kJ (39 Cal)

STEAMED PORK & PUMPKIN MONEY BAGS

100 g (3⅓ oz) peeled pumpkin,
chopped
100 g (3⅓ oz) pork or chicken
mince
1 egg white, lightly beaten
½ medium zucchini (courgette),
finely grated
16 won ton wrappers

1 Microwave or steam the pumpkin until soft, then mash until smooth.
2 Add the pork or chicken mince, egg white and zucchini and mix to combine.
3 Place 1 tablespoon of the filling in the center of each won ton wrapper. Brush the edges with water and gather together. Pinch the edges together to seal.
4 Place the money bags into a bamboo steamer lined with baking paper.
5 Put about 1 cup (250 ml/8 fl oz) of water into a wok. Sit the steamer over the water, cover the wok and steam the money bags for 7 minutes or until the meat is tender. Serve with your child's favourite dipping sauce. Makes 16

per money bag | fat 0.6 g | saturated fat 0.2 g | protein 2.4 g | carbohydrate 5 g | fibre 0.3 g | cholesterol 5 mg | energy 152 kJ (36 Cal)

steamed pork & pumpkin money bags

chicken nuggets with sweet potato stars

CHICKEN NUGGETS WITH SWEET POTATO STARS

1 Preheat oven to 200°C (400°F/Gas 6). Line
2 baking trays with baking paper.
2 Cut the chicken into bite-size pieces.
3 Dip the chicken into the beaten egg, toss to coat
in the cornflake crumbs and place on one of the
prepared trays.
4 Cut the sweet potato into 1 cm (½ in) thick slices
and use a star-shaped cutter to cut out stars. Place
on the second prepared tray.
5 Lightly spray the nuggets and the sweet potato
stars with olive oil spray. Bake the sweet potato
for 10 minutes, then add the nuggets and bake for
a further 10-15 minutes or until the nuggets are
tender and the sweet potato is soft. Serve with your
child's favourite dipping sauce. Serves 1-2

per serve (2) | **fat 8.9 g** | **saturated fat 2.5 g** | **protein
27.9 g** | **carbohydrate 33.7 g** | **fibre 2.2 g** | **cholesterol
160 mg** | **energy 1387 kJ (330 Cal)**

1 small skinless chicken breast
1 egg, lightly beaten
**½ cup (55 g/1²/₃ oz) cornflake
   crumbs**
**1 small (150 g/5 oz) orange sweet
   potato, peeled**
olive oil spray

CHICKEN NOODLE OMELETTE

½ packet (40 g/1⅓ oz) 2-minute
noodles (without flavour sachet)

1 egg, lightly beaten

1 tablespoon milk

1 tablespoon grated cheddar
cheese

2 tablespoons frozen peas and
corn, thawed

10 g (⅓ oz) butter or margarine

2 tablespoons shredded
barbecue chicken

1 Cook the noodles in a pan of boiling water for
2 minutes or until soft. Drain well.

2 Whisk together the egg, milk, cheese, peas and
corn, then add the noodles.

3 Melt the butter or margarine in a non-stick fry pan
over medium heat. Add the egg mixture, top with the
chicken and cook for 3-5 minutes or until just set.
Lift the edge during cooking to allow any unset egg
to run underneath.

4 Fold the omelette in half and slide out of the pan
and onto a plate. Delicious served hot or cold, with
salad. Serves 1-2

per serve (2) | fat 13.3 g | saturated fat 6.9 g | protein
10.1 g | carbohydrate 12.6 g | fibre 2.4 g | cholesterol
124 mg | energy 894 kJ (213 Cal)

chicken noodle omelette

TODDLER
DINNERS

vegetable macaroni cheese

VEGETABLE MACARONI CHEESE

30 g (1 oz) butter
1 tablespoon plain flour
1 cup (250 ml/8 fl oz) milk
1/4 cup (30 g/1 oz) grated carrot
1/4 cup (40 g/1 1/3 oz) grated
  zucchini (courgette)
1/4 cup (50 g/1 2/3 oz) corn kernels
50 g (1 2/3 oz) broccoli, cut into
  florets
1 cup (160 g/5 1/3 oz) cooked
  macaroni
1/2 cup (60 g/2 oz) grated
  cheddar cheese

1 Heat the butter in a pan over medium heat, add the flour and cook, stirring, for 1 minute.
2 Remove the pan from the heat and stir in the milk. Return to the heat and cook, stirring, until the sauce boils and thickens.
3 Add the vegetables and macaroni and cook for 5 minutes or until the vegetables are soft. Stir in the cheese and cook until it has melted. Serves 2-4
per serve (4) | fat 14 g | saturated fat 8.9 g | protein 9.2 g | carbohydrate 17.6 g | fibre 2.3 g | cholesterol 43 mg | energy 991 kJ (236 Cal)
* Store any leftover macaroni cheese in an airtight container in the refrigerator. Add a little extra milk or water when reheating.

FISH FINGERS & CHIPPIES

1 small (100 g/3 1/3 oz) boneless
  white fish fillet
1 egg, lightly beaten
1/2 cup (35 g/1 oz) dry or fresh
  breadcrumbs
1 medium potato, unpeeled
olive oil spray

1 Preheat oven to 220°C (425°F/Gas 7). Line a baking tray with baking paper.
2 Cut the fish into thick fingers. Dip into the egg and toss to coat in the breadcrumbs. Place the fish on the prepared tray.
3 Scrub the potato and cut it into wedges. Place on a non-stick baking tray.
4 Lightly spray the fish and potato with olive oil spray. Bake the potato for 30 minutes. Add the fish and cook for another 15 minutes or until the potato is crisp and golden and the fish is tender.
5 Serve the fish and chippies with tartare sauce for dipping. Serves 1
per serve | fat 8.3 g | saturated fat 2.2 g | protein 34.6 g | carbohydrate 43 g | fibre 4.4 g | cholesterol 283 mg | energy 1664 kJ (396 Cal)

fish fingers & chippies

kids' spaghetti

KIDS' SPAGHETTI

1 Cook the spaghetti in a large pan of rapidly boiling water until al dente (cooked, but still with a bite to it). Drain and keep warm.

2 Heat the oil in a non-stick fry pan, add the onion and cook over medium heat for 5 minutes or until soft and golden.

3 Add the beef and cook, stirring, for 5 minutes or until browned. Add the mushrooms and carrot and cook for 3 minutes or until soft.

4 Add the tomatoes and tomato sauce and bring to the boil. Reduce the heat and simmer for 15 minutes.

5 Spoon the spaghetti into a bowl, top with the sauce and sprinkle with the grated cheese. Serves 1-2

per serve (2) | fat 8.5 g | saturated fat 2.1 g | protein 10.8 g | carbohydrate 25 g | fibre 3.2 g | cholesterol 18 mg | energy 948 kJ (226 Cal)

50 g (1²/₃ oz) spaghetti
2 teaspoons oil
¹/₂ small onion, finely chopped
50 g (1²/₃ oz) lean beef mince
3 button mushrooms, chopped
¹/₂ small carrot, grated
200 g (6¹/₂ oz) can chopped tomatoes
1 tablespoon reduced-salt tomato sauce
1 tablespoon grated cheddar cheese

SPECIAL FRIED RICE

1 Heat the oil in a wok over medium heat, add the spring onion and ham and stir fry for 3 minutes or until the spring onion is soft.

2 Add the celery, carrot, capsicum and corn and stir fry for 5 minutes or until the vegetables are tender.

3 Add the rice and stir fry for 3 minutes or until heated through. Push the rice and vegetables to the side.

4 Add the egg and cook, stirring, until it is scrambled.

5 Pour in the soy sauce and stir fry with the rice, vegetables and egg for 1 minute. Serves 1-2

per serve (2) | fat 8.1 g | saturated fat 1.5 g | protein 9 g | carbohydrate 31.9 g | fibre 2.5 g | cholesterol 99 mg | energy 1012 kJ (241 Cal)

* You will need ¹/₃ cup (65 g/2 oz) uncooked rice.

2 teaspoons vegetable oil
1 spring onion (scallion), sliced
1 slice ham, chopped
¹/₂ celery stick, sliced
¹/₂ medium carrot, diced
¹/₄ small red capsicum (bell pepper), diced
¹/₄ cup (50 g/1²/₃ oz) corn kernels
1 cup (185 g/6 oz) cold cooked white rice*
1 egg, lightly beaten
1 teaspoon reduced-salt soy sauce

special fried rice

asian lamb noodles

ASIAN LAMB NOODLES

1 teaspoon canola oil

50 g (1²/₃ oz) lean lamb loin or
   fillet, cut into thin strips

1 cup (100 g/3¹/₃ oz) frozen
   stir fry vegetables (carrot,
   capsicum/bell pepper,
   snowpeas, broccoli)

2 tablespoons water

90 g (3 oz) fresh Hokkien noodles

2 teaspoons reduced-salt
   soy sauce

1 teaspoon honey

1 Heat the oil in a wok over medium heat. Add the lamb and stir fry for 3 minutes or until browned.
2 Add the vegetables and water and stir fry for 3 minutes or until the vegetables are just soft.
3 Add the noodles and the combined soy sauce and honey. Stir fry for 3 minutes or until the noodles soften. Serves 1-2

per serve (2) | **fat 3.5 g** | **saturated fat 0.6 g** | **protein 8.7 g** | **carbohydrate 17.6 g** | **fibre 2.7 g** | **cholesterol 16 mg** | **energy 597 kJ (142 Cal)**

SWEET CORN & CHICKEN NOODLE SOUP

130 g (4¹/₂ oz) can creamed corn

2 cups (500 ml/16 fl oz)
   reduced-salt chicken stock

1 tablespoon reduced-salt
   soy sauce

1 packet (80 g/2²/₃ oz) 2-minute
   noodles (without flavour sachet),
   broken into small pieces

¹/₂ cup (75 g/2¹/₂ oz) shredded
   barbecue chicken, with skin
   and bones removed

1 egg, lightly beaten

1 Put the creamed corn, stock and soy sauce into a pan and bring to the boil.
2 Break the noodles into small pieces, add to the soup and cook for 2 minutes or until soft.
3 Add the chicken and egg and stir until the egg floats to the surface. Cook for 5 minutes or until the chicken is heated through. Serve with toast. Makes 2¹/₂ cups (625 ml/20 fl oz)

per cup (250 ml/8 fl oz) | **fat 11.8 g** | **saturated fat 4.8 g** | **protein 17.5 g** | **carbohydrate 27.3 g** | **fibre 4.4 g** | **cholesterol 107 mg** | **energy 1229 kJ (293 Cal)**

sweet corn & chicken noodle soup

cheesy rissoles

CHEESY RISSOLES

1 Put the beef, onion, carrot, zucchini, tomato sauce, barbecue sauce, cheese and flour into a bowl and mix to combine.

2 Shape the mixture into 8 flat patties. Roll each patty in the breadcrumbs and place on a tray. Refrigerate for 15 minutes or until firm.

3 Heat the oil in a large non-stick fry pan over medium heat. Cook the patties in batches for 5-7 minutes on each side or until crisp and golden brown and cooked through. Drain on absorbent paper. Serve with tomato sauce and vegetables.

Makes 8

per rissole I **fat 9.1 g** I **saturated fat 3.3 g** I **protein 13.2 g** I **carbohydrate 8.2 g** I **fibre 0.8 g** I **cholesterol 33 mg** I **energy 705 kJ (168 Cal)**

* The rissoles can be frozen for up to a month before they are cooked.

400 g (13 oz) lean beef mince
1 small onion, grated
1 small carrot, grated
1 small zucchini (courgette), grated
2 tablespoons reduced-salt tomato sauce
1 tablespoon barbecue sauce
½ cup (60 g/2 oz) grated cheddar cheese
2 tablespoons plain flour
½ cup (35 g/1 oz) dry breadcrumbs
2 tablespoons canola oil

CREAMY POTATO FISH PIE

3 medium potatoes, peeled and
 chopped
1 cup (250 ml/8 fl oz) milk
1 small onion, grated
400 g (13 oz) firm boneless white
 fish fillets
20 g (3/4 oz) butter
1 tablespoon plain flour
1/4 cup (40 g/1 1/3 oz) frozen peas
1/4 cup (50 g/1 2/3 oz) corn kernels
1 tablespoon finely chopped
 fresh parsley
3/4 cup (90 g/3 oz) grated
 cheddar cheese

1 Preheat oven to 190°C (375°F/Gas 5).

2 Cook the potato in a pan of boiling water until tender. Drain well and mash.

3 Put the milk and onion into a large fry pan over medium heat, add the fish and gently simmer for 5-7 minutes or until the fish is tender and flakes when tested with the tip of a knife.

4 Drain the fish, reserving the liquid. Allow the fish to cool before flaking into small pieces.

5 Melt the butter in a small pan over medium heat, add the flour and cook for 1 minute or until golden. Remove from the heat and gradually stir in the reserved cooking liquid. Return the pan to the heat and cook, stirring constantly, until the sauce boils and thickens.

6 Add the peas, corn, parsley, fish and 1/2 cup (60 g/2 oz) of the cheese and cook until the cheese has melted.

7 Spoon the mixture into 4 x 1 cup (250 ml/8 fl oz) capacity ramekins or a 4 cup (1 litre/32 fl oz) capacity ovenproof dish. Top with the mashed potato and sprinkle with the remaining cheese. Bake for 20 minutes for the ramekins or 35 minutes for the ovenproof dish or until the top is golden brown. Serves 4

per serve | fat 15.2 g | saturated fat 9.4 g | protein 31.5 g | carbohydrate 21 g | fibre 2.9 g | cholesterol 139 mg | energy 1479 kJ (352 Cal)

* The pies can be frozen for up to 1 month. Thaw before reheating.

creamy potato fish pie

sticky chicken drumsticks

STICKY CHICKEN DRUMSTICKS

1 Preheat oven to 220°C (425°F/Gas 7).
2 Make 2 deep incisions on either side of each drumstick. Put the drumsticks into an ovenproof dish.
3 Put the tomato sauce, soy sauce and honey into a bowl and mix to combine. Pour over the chicken and set aside to marinate for 15 minutes.
4 Bake the chicken for 40-45 minutes or until tender. Serve with mashed potato and steamed vegetables.
Makes 4

per drumstick I fat 16.4 g I saturated fat 4.9 g
I protein 26.5 g I carbohydrate 7.3 g I fibre 0.1 g
I cholesterol 154 mg I energy 1174 kJ (280 Cal)
* Serve the drumsticks hot or cold. Cut the meat off the drumsticks and serve it in salads or sandwiches.

4 chicken drumsticks
1 tablespoon reduced-salt
  tomato sauce
1 tablespoon reduced-salt
  soy sauce
1 teaspoon honey

TUNA PATTIES

2 medium potatoes, peeled
   and chopped
1 cup (185 g/6 oz) cooked
   white rice*
2 spring onions (scallions),
   sliced
125 g (4 oz) can creamed corn
250 g (8 oz) can tuna in brine,
   drained
1 egg, lightly beaten
1 tablespoon plain flour
1/2 cup (35 g/1 oz) fresh
   breadcrumbs
1/4 cup (15 g/1/2 oz) dry
   breadcrumbs
2 tablespoons canola oil

1 Cook the potato in a pan of boiling water until tender. Drain well and mash.

2 Put the potato, rice, spring onions, creamed corn, tuna, egg, flour and fresh breadcrumbs into a bowl and mix to combine.

3 Shape the mixture into 8 flat patties. Roll each patty in the dry breadcrumbs and place on a tray. Refrigerate for 15 minutes or until firm.

4 Heat the oil in a large non-stick fry pan over medium heat. Cook the patties in batches for 3 minutes on each side or until crisp and golden brown and heated through. Drain on absorbent paper. Serve with salad. Makes 8

per patty | fat 4.9 g | saturated fat 0.7 g | **protein 9 g** | carbohydrate 19 g | fibre 1.6 g | cholesterol 35 mg | **energy 669 kJ (159 Cal)**

* You will need 1/3 cup (65 g/2 oz) uncooked rice. The patties can be frozen for up to a month before they are cooked.

tuna patties

TODDLER
SWEET TREATS

baked apple rice custards

BAKED APPLE RICE CUSTARDS

2 tablespoons cooked white rice

1 egg

2 teaspoons sugar

½ cup (125 ml/4 fl oz) milk or
reconstituted infant formula

140 g (4½ oz) apple puree

1 tablespoon sultanas

1 Preheat oven to 160°C (315°F/Gas 2-3).

2 Whisk together the rice, egg, sugar and milk.

3 Spoon the apple puree into 2 x ½ cup (125 ml/
4 fl oz) capacity ramekins and sprinkle with sultanas.

4 Pour the custard mixture over the apple puree and
sultanas. Put the ramekins into a baking dish and
pour in enough hot water to come halfway up the
sides of the ramekins. Bake for 30-40 minutes or
until the custard is just set. Serves 2

per serve | **fat 5.2 g** | **saturated fat 2.4 g** | **protein 6.1 g**
| **carbohydrate 23.9 g** | **fibre 2.6 g** | **cholesterol 102 mg**
| **energy 712 kJ (170 Cal)**

SOFT TOFU WITH BANANA & PASSIONFRUIT

100 g (3⅓ oz) silken tofu, drained

1 small banana, sliced

2 teaspoons passionfruit pulp

½ teaspoon pure maple syrup

1 Cut the tofu into small pieces and put into a bowl.

2 Top the tofu with the banana, passionfruit and
maple syrup. Serves 1

per serve | **fat 6.9 g** | **saturated fat 1 g** | **protein 13.6 g**
| **carbohydrate 20.2 g** | **fibre 5 g** | **cholesterol 0 mg**
| **energy 860 kJ (205 Cal)**

soft tofu with banana & passionfruit

fruit compote with yoghurt

FRUIT COMPOTE WITH YOGHURT

1 Put the apricots, prunes, apple, pear and orange juice into a pan and bring to the boil. Reduce the heat and simmer for 5-10 minutes or until the fruit is plump and nearly all the liquid has been absorbed.
2 Serve the fruit compote with the yoghurt. Serves 1
per serve | fat 1 g | saturated fat 0.4 g | protein 2.9 g | carbohydrate 51.9 g | fibre 6.8 g | cholesterol 3 mg | energy 984 kJ (234 Cal)
* To save time, use packaged dried fruit salad.

2 dried apricot halves
2 pitted prunes, roughly chopped
2 dried apple rings, halved
2 dried pear pieces, halved
½ cup (125 ml/4 fl oz) fresh
    orange juice
1 tablespoon no-added sugar
    apricot yoghurt

STEWED PEAR WITH CUSTARD

1 Peel and core the pear and cut it into quarters.
2 Put the pear and apple juice into a pan and bring to the boil. Reduce the heat, cover and simmer for 10 minutes. Remove the lid and cook for 5 minutes or until most of the liquid has been absorbed. Remove and set aside to cool.
3 Serve the stewed pear with the custard. Serves 1-2
per serve (2) | fat 0.7 g | saturated fat 0.5 g | protein 0.9 g | carbohydrate 23.8 g | fibre 1 g | cholesterol 2 mg | energy 439 kJ (104 Cal)

1 small pear
1 cup (250 ml/8 fl oz)
    unsweetened apple juice
2 tablespoons vanilla custard

stewed pear with custard

fruit jelly

FRUIT JELLY

**1 cup (250 ml/8 fl oz)
unsweetened apple juice**
1 teaspoon gelatin
**½ medium pear, peach or
apple, peeled and cut into
small shapes***

1 Put the apple juice and gelatin into a pan and stir over low heat until the gelatin dissolves and the juice is clear.
2 Divide the fruit between 2 x ½ cup (125 ml/ 4 fl oz) capacity ramekins or plastic cups. Pour in the apple juice mixture and refrigerate until set. Serves 2
per serve | fat 0.1 g | saturated fat 0 g | protein 1.6 g | carbohydrate 16.9 g | fibre 0.6 g | cholesterol 0 mg | energy 312 kJ (74 Cal)
* Any soft fruit can be used in the jelly. Try using canned fruit in natural juice in winter.

FROZEN FRUIT TREATS

1 kiwifruit
4 strawberries
**½ cup (85 g/2¾ oz) chopped
rockmelon**

1 Peel the kiwifruit and cut it into wedges. Halve the strawberries.
2 Thread the kiwifruit, strawberries and rockmelon onto 4 ice-cream sticks. Put the sticks onto a tray and freeze until firm. Makes 4
per stick | fat 0.1 g | saturated fat 0 g | protein 0.6 g | carbohydrate 3.2 g | fibre 1.1 g | cholesterol 0 mg | energy 78 kJ (19 Cal)

frozen fruit treats

layered yoghurt strawberry crunch

LAYERED YOGHURT STRAWBERRY CRUNCH

1 Slice half the strawberries and divide them between 2 glasses.

2 Top the strawberries with the yoghurt and drizzle with the honey.

3 Put the remaining strawberries into a blender and blend until smooth. Spoon the strawberry puree over the honey and top with the crushed biscuit. Serves 2

per serve | **fat 3 g** | **saturated fat 1.7 g** | **protein 3.8 g** | **carbohydrate 11.7 g** | **fibre 1.5 g** | **cholesterol 9 mg** | **energy 393 kJ (94 Cal)**

100 g (3^1/$_3$ oz) strawberries
100 g (3^1/$_3$ oz) plain yoghurt
1 teaspoon honey
1 shredded wheatmeal biscuit, crushed

FROZEN BABY CHOC BANANAS

1 Peel the bananas, thread them onto ice-cream sticks and put them onto a plate. Freeze the bananas until they are firm.

2 Drizzle the chocolate ice-cream coating over the frozen bananas. Makes 4

per choc banana | **fat 5.6 g** | **saturated fat 3.3 g** | **protein 2.5 g** | **carbohydrate 34.1 g** | **fibre 4.4 g** | **cholesterol 0 mg** | **energy 850 kJ (202 Cal)**

* Children will have fun drizzling the chocolate ice-cream coating over the bananas. If the chocolate coating is too hard for your children, chop the bananas and top them with some chocolate pudding dessert.

4 small ripe lady finger bananas
2 tablespoons chocolate ice-cream coating

frozen baby choc bananas

Publisher Jody Vassallo
General manager Claire Connolly
Recipes & styling Jody Vassallo
Photographer Ben Dearnley
Home economist Penelope Grieve
Recipe testing Penelope Grieve
Props stylists Melissa Singer, Trish Hegarty
Designer Annette Fitzgerald
Editor Justine Harding
Consultant dietitian Dr Susanna Holt

STYLING CREDITS:
Design Mode International (02) 9998 8200
Dinosaur Designs (02) 9361 3776
Freedom Furniture (02) 9948 0238
Target (02) 8440 5300
Toys R Us (02) 9413 2970
Wheel & Barrow (02) 9938 4555
Appliances used in this book provided by
Sunbeam Corporation Limited.
© **Recipes** Jody Vassallo 2003
© **Photography** Ben Dearnley 2003
© **Series design** Fortiori Publishing

Print management Steve Allan, Web Production

PUBLISHED BY FORTIORI PUBLISHING:
PO Box 126 Nunawading BC
Victoria 3110 Australia
Phone: 61 3 9872 3855
Fax: 61 3 9872 5454
salesenquiries@fortiori.com.au
www.fortiori.com.au
order direct on (03) 9872 3855

Printed by McPherson's Printing Group.
Printed in Australia.

ISBN 0 9581609 6 1

DISCLAIMER: The nutritional information listed under each recipe does not include the nutrient content of garnishes or any accompaniments not listed in specific quantities in the ingredient list. The nutritional information for each recipe is an estimate only, and may vary depending on the brand of ingredients used, and due to natural biological variations in the composition of natural foods such as meat, fish, fruit and vegetables. The nutritional information was calculated by a qualified dietitian using FoodWorks dietary analysis software (Professional Version 3.10, Xyris Software Pty Ltd, Highgate Hill, Queensland, Australia) based on the Australian food composition tables and food manufacturers' data. Where not specified, ingredients are analysed as average or medium. All recipes were analysed using 59 g eggs.

IMPORTANT: Those who might suffer particularly adverse effects from salmonella food poisoning (the elderly, pregnant women, young children and those with immune system problems) should consult their general practitioner about consuming raw or undercooked eggs.